THE EXCHANGE

JEFF MUSGRAVE

LEADER'S GUIDE

the
exchange

The Exchange Leader's Guide
© 2016 by Jeff Musgrave

ISBN: 978-1-94429-805-0

Cover Design by Justin Hall
Interior Design by Niddy Griddy Design, Inc.

Unless otherwise noted, all Scripture is quoted from The Holy Bible, King James Version (KJV), Public Domain.

1 2 3 4 5 6 7 8 9 10 Printing / Year 19 18 17 16

Contents

Introduction v

Lesson 1 God Is Holy 1

Lesson 2 God Is Just 15

Lesson 3 God Is Loving 27

Lesson 4 God Is Gracious 43

Introduction

Early in Jesus' earthly ministry, two of John's disciples asked Jesus where He lived. He did not reply with directions to the place. He simply said to them, "Come and see" (John 1:39). Do you see how relational that is? Six verses later Philip, one of Jesus' disciples, wanted to tell his friend Nathaniel about Jesus. When Philip told his friend that Jesus was the Messiah, Nathaniel was not impressed. He replied, "Can any good thing come out of Nazareth?" So Philip pulled out his apologetics book, and began to tell his friend that Jesus was really born in Bethlehem, fulfilled 15 Old Testament prophecies....

That's not what Philip did. He simply invited his friend to, "Come and see." Philip knew that if his friend met Jesus firsthand and got to know Him like he knew Jesus, Nathaniel would love Him as much as he did. Evangelism is more than just dispensing information. Evangelism, at its core, is relational. It's about you having a close and growing relationship with Jesus, caring about your friend enough to grow closer to him, and introducing your friend to your best Friend.

HERE'S HOW I VIEW *THE EXCHANGE*

Imagine the excitement of a young man introducing the girl of his dreams to everyone he knows. "Not only is she perfect," he might say, "but she loves me!" This excitement parallels my desire to introduce Jesus to you. He has become my very best friend, and He can become yours, too. However, there are some very troubling misconceptions about Him and I want you to know Him as He really is, not as others may have portrayed Him to you. Please understand, I don't mean my idea of Him versus others' ideas of Him. I want to introduce Him to you from the Bible so that you can get to know Him for yourself.

Jesus is such an intriguing Person! Where do I begin? He is both complex and simple. There is so much I don't know about Him, yet His friendship is the most comforting aspect of my life. He is perfect—literally, unlike anyone you've ever known or will know. He is the most loyal, true Person you will ever meet. His nature is such that He cannot relate to us in our current condition. Yet, His love for us is so great He has gone to extreme measures to form a relationship with us. He has stretched out His love across the vast differences between our nature and His, making possible an eternal, satisfying relationship with Him. He is invisible, eternal and all-powerful and through a simple gift, He has placed eternity within our grasp. Man may try to find another way to an eternal place in heaven, but there is no other way.

To get to know a person you must spend time together, asking questions that help you to understand what that person is really like. In a similar manner, you probably have many questions you would like to ask God. In the Bible we find answers to our questions about God. The Bible is a series of books from God to men, in which He reveals Himself to mankind so that we might know Him. I invite you to do a four-lesson Bible study that will introduce God to you and show you how to have a meaningful relationship with Him, bringing peace and purpose to your life.

WHY THE BIBLE STUDY WORKS

The Power of the Word of God

The Exchange Bible study is designed to introduce your friend to the living God of the Bible. An unbeliever need not profess confidence in the Bible before examining and investigating its claims. *The Exchange* makes no attempt to prove the veracity of the Word of God or even the existence of God. Confidence in the self-authenticating nature of the Bible and the power of the gospel message drives this approach.

"Do I have to believe this Adam and Eve stuff to have a relationship with this God of yours?" This was Karlton's first question. He felt God was a crutch, a figment of weak men's imagination. Though skeptical, Karlton's questions were sincere. At the end of our first conversation, he and his wife, Michelle, agreed to do *The Exchange* Bible study.

As we finished our first study, Michelle apologized for Karlton's skepticism and my wife wondered if we should get him an apologetics book that might lend some credibility to our witness. However, we decided to stay the course and let the gospel show itself powerful in Karlton's life.

Our second Bible study was slightly better. Instead of saying, "That can't be true because…" he was saying, "Well, if that's true, what about…?" Before we could study the third lesson, Karlton said to me, "I don't need to finish the Bible study. I know it's true. I want to make that exchange you've been telling me about." Today Karlton and his family continue to grow in their walk with Christ.

The Bible is powerful. Consider the story of the rich man and Lazarus. The rich man feared that his brothers would not listen to the warning of coming judgment found in the Word of God, so he pled with Abraham to have Lazarus rise from dead and warn his brothers about Hell. Abraham answered by telling him that the Word of God is the most powerful tool we have to persuade men of the truth of Hell and the gift of eternal life found in Jesus.

> Luke 16:31 And he said unto him, If they hear not Moses and the prophets, neither will they be persuaded, though one rose from the dead.

In His great high priestly prayer, Jesus declared the Word of God to be absolute truth, and demonstrated His confidence in its redemptive power.

> John 17:17 Sanctify them through *your* truth: *your* word is truth.

Jesus promised that the truth gives freedom from the slavery of sin.

> John 8:32, 34 And *you* shall know the truth, and the truth shall make you free. … Verily, verily, I say unto you, *Whoever commits* sin is the servant [slave] of sin.

JESUS IS LIFE AND USES THE BIBLE TO IMPART HIS LIFE TO MEN

> John 1:4 In him was life; and the life was the light of men.

> Hebrews 4:12 For the word of God is quick [alive], and powerful, and sharper than any twoedged sword, piercing even to the dividing asunder of soul and spirit, and of the joints and marrow, and is a discerner of the thoughts and intents of the heart.

> Romans 10:17 So then faith *comes* by hearing, and hearing by the word of God.

> Isaiah 55:10–11 For as the rain *comes* down, and … *waters* the earth, and *makes* it bring forth and bud, … So shall my word be that *goes* forth out of my mouth: it shall not return unto me void, but it shall accomplish that which I please, and it shall prosper in the thing whereto I sent it.

We can expect this lifesaving truth to be accepted by some and rejected by others.

> John 6:44 No man can come to me, except the Father which *has* sent me draw him.

> John 8:45, 47 "And because I tell you the truth, *you* believe me not.... He that is of God *hears* God's words: *you* therefore hear them not, because *you* are not of God.

> John 1:11–12 He came unto his own, and his own received him not. But as many as received him, to them gave he power to become the sons of God, even to them that believe on his name.

The Promises of the Word of God

The Exchange is a simple, straightforward presentation of the four aspects of God's character that reveal both the need and provision of His great salvation for mankind. This introduction to God as a person is somewhat inductive in style by gradually unveiling the truth of the gospel. While *The Exchange* is engaging and compelling, the power of the gospel is what makes it effective.

> Romans 1:16 For I am not ashamed of the gospel of Christ: for it is the power of God unto salvation to every one that *believes*.

We need not try to prove the claims of the Bible. We can patiently allow our friend to discover these truths for himself because we can trust the promise of the Spirit to convince him.

> John 16:8 And when he is come, he will reprove [convince] the world of sin, and of righteousness, and of judgment.

We can also expect our friend's journey into truth to be hindered by the enemy.

> 2 Corinthians 4:4 In whom the god of this world *has* blinded the minds of them which believe not, lest the light of the glorious gospel of Christ, who is the image of God, should shine unto them.

> Matthew 13:19 When any one *hears* the word of the kingdom, and *understands* it not, then *comes* the wicked one, and *catches* away that which was sown in his heart.

So we must stay attentive to the needs of our friend and actively engaged in the spiritual battle for his soul.

> 2 Corinthians 5:20 Now then we are ambassadors for Christ, as though God did beseech you by us: we pray you in Christ's stead, be *you* reconciled to God.

Because God has promised a plentiful harvest, if we are diligently working in our Father's fields, we can be confident we will see souls saved and lives transformed by and for the glory of God.

> John 4:35 Say not *you*, There are yet four months, and then *comes* harvest? behold, I say unto you, Lift up your eyes, and look on the fields; for they are white already to harvest.

> 1 Corinthians 9:22 I am made all things to all men, that I might by all means save some.

The urgent need of our day is for bold laborers.

> Matthew 9:37–38 Then *said* he unto his disciples, The harvest truly is plenteous, but the labourers are few; Pray *you* therefore the Lord of the harvest, that he will send forth labourers into his harvest.

BIBLICAL BOLDNESS IN EVANGELISM AND DISCIPLESHIP

The early church rarely prayed that God would work in the hearts of the lost. They were confident He was doing that work. They didn't attempt to pray God down or stir Him up. Their constant cry was for personal boldness. Even the apostle Paul, one of the boldest men who has ever lived, felt the need to pray for boldness.

> Ephesians 6:18–20 Praying always with all prayer and supplication in the Spirit, and watching thereunto with all perseverance and supplication for all saints; And for me, that utterance may be given unto me, that I may open my mouth boldly, to make known the mystery [hidden truth] of the gospel, For which I am an ambassador in bonds: that therein I may speak boldly, as I ought to speak.

Boldness was a key character trait in the early church. The word is used ten times in the book of Acts and thirty-one times from Acts to Revelation.

> Acts 4:13 Now when they saw the boldness of Peter and John, and perceived that they were unlearned and ignorant men, they marvelled; and they took knowledge of them, that they had been with Jesus.

> Acts 4:29 And now, Lord, behold their threatenings: and grant unto *your* servants, that with all boldness they may speak *your* word.

> Acts 28:31 Preaching the kingdom of God, and teaching those things which concern the Lord Jesus Christ, with all confidence, no man forbidding him.

There is a difference between boldness and brashness. Imagine being given the responsibility of standing on a stretch of road to warn all oncoming traffic, "Stop! You can't go this way!" Now imagine the same scenario, but this time the message is "Stop! You can't go this way! The bridge is out!" Would you perceive and approach the job differently?

Boldness comes from a conscious awareness of impending judgment and from sharing our Savior's compassion.

> Matthew 25:41, 46 Then shall he say also unto them on the left hand, Depart from me, *you* cursed, into everlasting fire, prepared for the devil and his angels. ... And these shall go away into everlasting punishment: but the righteous into life eternal.

> Matthew 9:36 But when he saw the multitudes, he was moved with compassion on them, because they fainted, and were scattered abroad, as sheep having no shepherd.

The Lord's clear commands ought to motivate us to be bold.

> Mark 16:15 And he said unto them, Go ... into all the world, and preach the gospel to every creature.

Boldness comes from confidence in the gospel and knowing that we cooperate with the Spirit of God.

> Romans 1:16 For I am not ashamed of the gospel of Christ: for it is the power of God unto salvation to every one that *believes;* to the Jew first, and also to the Greek.

> 2 Corinthians 10:3–5 For though we walk in the flesh, we do not war after the flesh: (For the weapons of our warfare are not carnal, but mighty through God to the pulling down of strong holds;) Casting down imaginations, and every high thing that *exalts* itself against the knowledge of God, and bringing into captivity every thought to the obedience of Christ.

> Acts 1:8 But *you* shall receive power, after that the Holy Ghost is come upon you: and *you* shall be witnesses unto me.

A divine appointment is when God providentially enables you to touch a life in which He has already been working. The pages of Scripture are permeated with divine appointments. Evangelism is not drumming up business or selling people on our religion. When we are convinced that God is drawing people to Himself, evangelism becomes a great treasure hunt. Your boldness will increase as you focus on Divine Appointments.

> Acts 18:9–10 Then spoke the Lord to Paul in the night by a vision, Be not afraid, but speak, and hold not *your* peace: For I am with *you,* and no man shall set on *you* to hurt *you*: for I have much people in this city.

> 2 Timothy 2:24-26 And the servant of the Lord must not strive; but be gentle unto all men, apt to teach, patient, In meekness instructing those that oppose themselves; if God peradventure will give them repentance to the acknowledging of the truth; And that they may recover themselves out of the snare of the devil, who are taken captive by him at his will.

As we continually pray for open doors, divine appointments and boldness, we will go through each day expecting to find people to invite to "come and see" Jesus.

> Colossians 4:2–4 Continue in prayer, and watch in the same with thanksgiving; Withal praying also for us, that God would open unto us a door of utterance, to speak the mystery of Christ, for which I am also in bonds: That I may make it manifest, as I ought to speak.

TIPS FOR SUCCESS

The Exchange Bible study is designed for your friend to study each lesson independently and then meet with you to discuss what he is learning. You should schedule about one hour per lesson. It only takes about thirty minutes to read each lesson out loud while answering the questions. Some will have more questions and discussion than others, but an hour is usually sufficient.

Relationship

Do the Bible study in the context of a warm relationship. If your friendship is not currently strong, invest time getting to know each other better. Find the connecting points between your lives in an effort to draw closer to your friend. She is much more likely to say yes when you have a good relationship.

Positive

Be positive and confident when you invite a friend to do the Bible study. You can assure him that he'll really enjoy the Bible study because you are going to make it an enjoyable experience.

Initiative

Take the initiative. Don't give the Bible study to your friend and ask him to think about it and get back with you. If he needs time to think about it, take it upon yourself to contact him at an appropriate time. Be the leader!

Time

Set a time for the Bible study when you give it to her. *The Exchange* has a short shelf life. The devil is eager to snatch away the seed.

Homework

Explain that she can do the Bible study ahead of time if she would like, but if she doesn't have time you can do it together when you meet. The last thing you want is for her to cancel because she didn't get her "homework" done. About half the people do the Bible study ahead of time and half don't and it doesn't seem to affect the outcome at all. Some people may not want you looking over their shoulder when they're trying to answer. They'll probably do it ahead of time. Others may think, "Do it together? That sounds good." They may be just as interested; they just show it differently.

Answers

Do your own Bible study ahead of time, carefully completing each answer. The Bible study impacts people more powerfully when they interact with it rather than just reading it. If your friend has read it but not filled in the answers, it is a good idea to read it together, giving him time to fill in the blanks or answer each question verbally. Avoid answering the questions for him. Allow him to extract truth for himself. If he has filled out the answers, there is no need to reread the entire lesson. Use the discussion questions in the sidebars to help you lead a discussion about the lesson.

In Your Own Words

The answers are in bold print. You can write the bold words in the blank, but it is much more impacting to reword the answer in your own words.

Discussion

Don't let your time together become a monologue in which you do all the talking. This is not a preaching time—it's a Bible study. The object of each session is to have a discussion. Your purpose is to discover and meet your friend's needs. If you listen and give him plenty of opportunities to discuss his thoughts, you'll discover your friend's questions and any obstacles that may be hindering his faith. By listening, you'll discover what is going on in his heart.

Use the questions and comments in the sidebars to help you lead your discussions.

Be Transparent

Some of the questions will probe into the personal life of your friend. He will more readily open his heart if you pave the way by admitting your own weaknesses and problems. None of us is perfect. You have more in common with the struggles of your unsaved friend than you might realize.

> 1 Corinthians 10:13 There *has* no temptation taken you but such as is common to man: but God is faithful, who will not suffer you to be tempted above that *you* are able; but will with the temptation also make a way to escape, that *you* may be able to bear it.

Setting

Do the Bible study in a setting that is comfortable for your friend. Consider doing it in your friend's home so that all that has to happen for the Bible study to take place is that you show up. Many have found a coffee shop or quiet restaurant to be a comfortable setting.

Reminder

Don't call to remind her of the Bible study. Just show up. A reminder call might provide an opportunity for her to cancel. Have you ever made a commitment to do something but contemplated canceling because you got busy or nervous? Your friend might be thinking the same thing.

Don't Give Up

Keep doing the Bible study even if it seems your friend is losing interest, it gets difficult to schedule a lesson, or even if a lesson gets uncomfortable. Sometimes it takes a long time to finish *The Exchange*, but some of the most glorious outcomes have come from challenging Bible studies. Only quit if your friend actually tells you he no longer wants to finish.

> Galatians 6:9 And let us not be weary in well doing: for in due season we shall reap, if we faint not.

Food

You could call this the ministry of food. Consider having dinner together before you study, or bring dessert. Food seems to draw people together. Jesus loved to spend time with people around the table.

Patience

Remember, your friend is discovering the truth for herself. This takes time. She may not always answer correctly. Don't worry. Just give God's Spirit time to work through the Scripture.

Goal

Show your own growing awe of your awesome God. Leave each lesson with the confidence that your friend understood the main theme of each lesson.

"Expect great things from God. Attempt great things for God." — William Carey

WHO CAN I INVITE?

Relationships are the catalyst for Evangelism Opportunities

Use this simple acrostic to help you find people in your sphere of influence that you might be able to engage in redemptive relationships.

Friends and Family
Associates from work, sports teams, clubs, the gym, your barber, dentist, etc.
Neighbors—Those who live next door and across the street, people you meet in your community as you take
      walks, visit the coffee shop, grocery, bank, etc.
Strangers—Ask God to bring new people into your life and help you connect with them.
      Engage them in conversation,
      Connect with them on a deeper level, and then
      Invite them to do *The Exchange*.

NOTE: As your friends and acquaintances go through traumatic events such as illness, divorce, the loss of a loved one, or other major changes, remember that in these difficult times people are often more receptive to the gospel. Your expressions of love and concern will often lead to an opportunity to do *The Exchange* together.

Keep a list of at least 5 people with whom you are intentionally cultivating relationships. Look for open doors to do *The Exchange*.

Be creative!

Look for ways to build relationships that will lead to gospel opportunities.

> e.g.—Work out at a gym; join a club; volunteer at a hospital, crisis pregnancy center, shelter, community assistance center, pet shelter—anywhere you will be working side by side with people.

Church services or fellowships are great places to meet people who need the gospel.

> In today's world, people may not make a decision for Christ at church or an event. But an invitation to get together socially may open the door to ultimately do *The Exchange* together.

Invite several friends for a group Bible study.

> Encourage your Christian friends to include unsaved friends. Provide plenty of opportunities for unbelievers to contribute to the discussion. Believers who have all the answers or use Christian "lingo" can easily intimidate unbelievers.

Turning a conversation to the gospel is more of a 3-point turn than a U-turn.

> It is easier to direct the conversation to a spiritual or religious topic and then direct it to the gospel from there.

Here is one way to invite a friend to do *The Exchange*.

> "Have you ever wondered if there really is a God and what He's like? I have a simple four lesson Bible study …"

⬡ God Is Holy

One of the most damaging notions to a real understanding of God and His relationship with man is the concept that God is a force or an energy source. While God is indeed a force with which to be reckoned and the greatest power in the universe, He is so much more than that. He is a person! When we remove the concept of His personhood from our thinking, we take away the fact that He has likes and dislikes. We hinder our ability to understand the whole concept of morality. We are left to define all the great questions of life by our own experience and intellect. This Bible study will not attempt to do that. Instead, this is an introduction to God as a person. Once you get to know Him as a person, you will have access to Him—the Source of all the answers to life's great questions.

The Bible is a series of books from God to men in which He reveals Himself to mankind so that we may know Him.

1. Some people have the misconception that the Bible can be interpreted any way a person chooses. Notice what the Bible says about private interpretations.

> 2 Peter 1:20–21 Knowing this first, that ᵃ**no prophecy of the scripture is of any private interpretation.** ᵇ**For the prophecy came not** in old time **by the will of man**: but ᶜ**holy men of God** *spoke* **as they were moved by the Holy Ghost [Spirit].***

1

What do you think of the Bible study so far?

What questions do you have?

What did you learn that you didn't already know?

What impacted you most in this lesson?

What do you think about God being a person Who has likes and dislikes?

Can you think of one way this truth might impact your life? (Does God like everything you do? Morality is based on God's character.)

How did the Bible get to us? (The Bible is not subject to personal interpretations. Each passage has a specific message from God to men. It is not hard to understand, just hard to obey.)

Do you think people tend to impose their own ideas on the Bible?

Why do you think some people want to alter the message of the Bible?

The Bible never tries to prove the existence of God.

THE EXCHANGE

a. What does the Bible say about private interpretations?

_____

_____

b. Why is it wrong to make the Bible say what we want it to say?

_____

c. According to this verse, who wrote the Bible?

_____

The Bible was written by God's Holy Spirit, Who directed holy men to communicate His message to mankind. The "private interpretation" mentioned in this verse is probably not aimed at the reader so much as it is a record of how the Bible got to us. The Bible is not the personal opinions of the human writers but the revelation of God. As such, there is a message from God that must be discovered without putting our own ideas or thoughts into it.

This is a Bible study. The purpose of this study is to lead you to a personal understanding of what the Bible says about God—to see it for yourself. A wise man once said, "The Bible is not hard to understand. It's just hard to obey." If at any point along the way you do not understand or agree, please do not hesitate to discuss your concern with your Bible study leader. You may not agree with everything the Bible says, but at least we should be able to come to an agreement about what the Bible teaches.

The Bible presupposes the existence of God and tells us from the very beginning Who He is.

> Genesis 1:1 In the beginning God

In these four Bible lessons, we will examine four of God's greatest attributes—God is holy, God is just, God is loving, and God is gracious and merciful. God's holiness is mentioned nearly twice as often in the Bible as any of His other attributes.

2

---

2. The Bible gives us only two glimpses into the actual throne room of God. What phrase are the angels calling to each other in awe of His presence?

> Isaiah 6:1–3 In the year that king Uzziah died I saw also the LORD sitting upon a throne, high and lifted up, and his *train filled the temple. Above it stood the seraphims [angels]: each one had six wings; with *two* he covered his face, and with *two* he covered his feet, and with *two* he did fly. And one cried unto another, and said, **Holy, holy, holy, is the LORD of hosts: the whole earth is full of his glory.**

Ask your friend to picture Heaven and all its beauty as you read these verses.

_____

*God's visible aura filled the temple.

3. The next glimpse into this room is in the last book of the Bible. The event described takes place at least 2,600 years after the one in Isaiah 6. What phrase is still the angels' ceaseless cry to each other?

> Revelation 4:8 And the four beasts [angels] had each of them six wings about him; and they were full of eyes within: and they rest not day and night, saying, **Holy, holy, holy, LORD God Almighty, which was, and is, and is to come.**

Comment on the wonder of this ongoing praise. (Think about it: either those angels are getting tired by now, or God's holiness is so awesome that the angels can't help but respond to His presence with cries of praise even after 2,600 years of doing so.)

_____

The word *holy* means "separate" or "set apart." It has come to carry with it the idea of separation from the imperfections of sin. God is sinless. He has never done anything wrong.

How would you define *holy* now that you have read these passages? (Perfect, unique, separate from all else, gloriously beautiful, righteous, always doing right. God cannot act in a way that is contrary to His nature.)

4. In the Bible God declares Himself holy. What responsibility is placed on man as a result of God's holy nature?

> Leviticus 11:44 For I am the LORD your God: *you* shall therefore *sanctify yourselves, and **you shall be holy; for I am holy.**

_____

3

We've never seen anything as beautiful as God's perfectly pristine glory.

Does God ever make mistakes or do wrong?

Has there ever been a time in your life when you questioned His goodness? (Some things won't be totally understood until after God's final judgment.)

★ Sometimes we cannot change our circumstances, but we can change our view of them. We can learn to evaluate our circumstances in the light of God's Word rather than evaluating God's Word in the light of our circumstances.

How does this truth about God impact you? (He keeps all His promises. He will never leave me. He will always do what is best.)

Is there anyone holy like God is holy?

THE EXCHANGE

5. What word did Jesus use to define God's holiness?

> Matthew 5:48 Be ... therefore **perfect,** even as your Father which is in heaven is **perfect.**

God is perfect! He is separate from everything. God's holiness is best defined as His uniqueness. He is holy! There is no one else like Him. His holiness is described as "beautiful" many times in the Bible. His holy nature is gloriously beautiful. Another word used in close association with His holiness is *righteous*. You can count on the fact that God will always do the right thing. He is perfectly righteous. The idea is that of fulfilling a contract completely or perfectly. There may be times when we do not think that He is doing what is right, but He is holy. We are not. He always does what is right. He is not only the ruler of all and not answerable to you and me, but He will always do the right thing. He has to. It is His character, His nature to do so; and He cannot violate His nature.

6. When a person doesn't know God, does it change Who God is and what He expects from man?

> Isaiah 45:5 **I am the LORD, and there is none else,** there is no God beside me: I girded [strengthened] *you*, **though *you have not known me.***

---

7. Who does the Bible say is holy like God is holy?

> 1 Samuel 2:2 **There is none holy** as the LORD: for there is none beside *you*: neither is there any rock like our God.

You may be familiar with the Ten Commandments. God's law is a reflection of His nature and the essence of sin is offending His holy nature. The Ten Commandments are not just rules to live by. Each

4

commandment protects us from offending Him. When we break God's law, we distance ourselves from Him.

8. Read the record of the first giving of the Ten Commandments.

> Exodus 20:1–17 And [a]**God** *spoke* all these words, saying, **I am the** L*ord* *your* **God,** which have brought *you* out of the land of Egypt, out of the house of bondage.

I.   [b]*You shall* have no other gods before me.

II.   *You shall* not make *to yourself* any graven image, or any likeness of any thing that is in heaven above, or that is in the earth beneath, or that is in the water under the earth. *You shall* not bow down *yourself* to them, nor serve them: for [c]**I the** L*ord* *your* **God am a jealous God,** visiting the iniquity of the fathers upon the children unto the third and fourth generation of them that hate me; And shewing mercy unto thousands of them that love me, and keep my commandments.

III.   [d]*You shall* not take the name of the L*ord* *your* God in vain; for [f]the L*ord* will not hold him guiltless that *takes* his name in vain.

IV.   Remember the sabbath day, to keep it holy. Six days *shall you* labour, and do all *your* work: But the seventh day is the sabbath of the L*ord* *your* God: in it *you shall* not do any work.

V.   Honour *your* father and *your* mother: that *your* days may be long upon the land which the L*ord* *your* God *gives you.*

VI.   *You shall* not kill.

VII.   *You shall* not commit adultery.

VIII.   *You shall* not steal.

★ Emphasize that God's commandments reveal His character. They are not arbitrary rules to "hem us in." They are a reflection of His nature. As a reflection of Gods holy nature, each law protects us from offending Him. When we break God's Law we distance ourselves from Him.

5

There is no one like God. He is unique; He is holy. When we value something more than God, we offend Him.

What do you think about this statement from God?—"I the Lord your God am a jealous God."

★ Jealousy is a love word. God is faithful in His love to us and expects us to be faithful to Him. Jealousy is a loving response to unfaithfulness. One of the names God uses to describe Himself is El Kana—The Jealous God. He uses this name to reveal His passionate, zealous love for us. He longs to have a relationship with us built on faithfulness and truth.

THE EXCHANGE

IX. *You shall* not bear false witness against *your* neighbour.

X. *You shall* not covet *your* neighbour's house, *you shall* not covet *your* neighbour's wife, nor his manservant, nor his maidservant, nor his ox, nor his *donkey,* nor any thing that is *your* neighbour's.

a. Who gave us the Ten Commandments and what did He call Himself?

_____

(The answer is found in Exodus 20:1 on page 5.)

b. What major attribute of God does the first commandment reflect?

_____

God is unique; there is no one like Him. He is holy.

c. What attribute of God demands that we have no idols in our lives? An idol is anything that is more important to us than God.

_____

Jealous is a love word. God is faithful in His love to us and expects us to be faithful to Him.

d. What do you think taking God's name "in vain" is?

_____

To take His name in vain is to use it flippantly or as an expletive like "Oh my _____!" (or "OMG").

6

e. Have you ever taken God's name in vain?

_____

f. What do you think this phrase means?—"the Lord will not hold him guiltless"

_____

One of the aspects of God's holiness is not just that He simply dislikes sin, but that He cannot tolerate it. It is not just that He will not, but that He cannot. He cannot deny any part of His perfect nature.

> Habakkuk 1:13 *You* [God] *are* of purer eyes than to behold evil, and *cannot* look on iniquity [sin].

There are as many definitions for right and wrong as there are people. Remember, we said that knowing God as a person clarifies some of these things. Sin is defined by God's holy nature and His definition is the only one that counts.

> 1 John 3:4 Sin is the trangression [breaking] of the law.

No one likes to be told what to do, and at the core of sin is our rebellion against God's law. When we sin, it is not simply that we have hurt someone or something; it is that we have offended God's holy nature.

g. How would you define "Honor your father and mother"?

_____

To honor is not just obedience, but having and displaying a sweet spirit at all times. Have you ever broken this command? There probably isn't a person alive who hasn't, especially in his teen years. The Bible calls that offense to God's holy nature "sin." You have broken God's law!

7

★ In the Old Testament, a priest who entered the holy place of God without first taking care of his sin would die.

If a bottle of water was perfectly pure except for one drop of toxic waste, would you drink it? No! You know the danger of toxic waste and God knows the danger of sin.

How would you explain this phrase?—"God cannot look on sin." (God cannot allow sin to remain in His presence. If I stand before God with sin in my life, He must remove me.)

What is sin? (Sin is rebellion against God's sovereign rule over us. Sin is offending God's holy nature.)

★ What are some "extreme" sins; now what are some sins that everyone has done?

Extreme Sins	Common Sins
Murder	Lying
Adultery	Lust
Treason	Disloyalty
Robbery	Cheating on taxes

Which of these sins separate us from God? (All of them)

★ Covet—wanting what God has not chosen to give you.

Which of God's characteristics reflected by the Ten Commandments has impacted you most?

Have you ever broken any of the Ten Commandments?

Have you ever broken any of God's Laws?

Has anyone ever escaped this problem of offending God by sinning?

THE EXCHANGE

God created the family to teach us how to love and respect Him through learning to love and respect our parents.

God's command not to **murder** is a reflection of His love for human life. He created and sustains all that lives.

> Colossians 1:16–17 For by him were all things created, that are in heaven, and that are in earth, visible and invisible ... all things were created by him, and for him: And he is before all things, and by him all things consist.

His command not to **commit adultery** is a reflection of His loyalty and faithfulness. God is committed to the institution of marriage.

> Hebrews 13:4 Marriage is honourable in all, and the bed undefiled: but *whoremongers and adulterers God will judge.

His command not to **steal** shows Him as the provider of all material blessings.

> Matthew 5:45 Your Father... *makes* his sun to rise on the evil and on the good, and *sends* rain on the just and on the unjust.

His command not to **lie** reflects His truthful nature. In fact, Titus 1:2 teaches that He cannot lie!

> Numbers 23:19 God is not a man, that he should lie.

His command not to **covet** shows that God holds us responsible for what is in our hearts as well as what is in our conduct.

Have you ever lied? Have you ever committed adultery or stolen or coveted? You've broken God's law. You've offended His holy nature. Offending God's nature is the very essence of sin.

8

9. Has anyone ever escaped this problem of sin?

> Ecclesiastes 7:20 **There is not a** just **man** upon earth, **that** *does* good, and *sins* **not.**

_____

Most of us are willing to admit that we have sinned, but many do not know that because of God's holy nature, sin disqualifies us from having a relationship with God.

10. What does this verse say is true about every person who has ever lived?

> Romans 3:23 For **all have sinned,** and **come short of the glory of God.**

_____

Imagine for a moment that you and your Bible study leader are standing on the edge of the Grand Canyon. As you look across the eight-mile span to the other side, you are impressed not only by the distance to the other side but also by the nearly one-mile drop to the canyon floor below. What would happen if you had a contest to see which one of you could jump across? It would be foolish and futile. One of you would probably jump farther than the other, but you would both fall short of the other side. The Bible teaches us the same thing is true about our relationship with God. Some people may sin less than others, but all of us have sinned and have fallen short of God's standard of holy perfection.

11. How many sins does it take to keep a person out of God's Heaven?

> Revelation 21:27 And there shall in no wise enter into it [Heaven] **any thing that** *defiles*, neither *whatever works* abomination, or *makes* **a lie:** but they which are written in the Lamb's book of life.

_____

9

How would you describe falling short of the glory of God? (The Grand Canyon illustration helps us see that no one can meet God's standard of perfection or holiness.)

We can feel pretty good about ourselves when we compare ourselves with other people, but when we compare ourselves to God's holiness, we all fall short.

★ Visualize this illustration together so that your friend understands that the distance between God and us is too great. We cannot bridge that gap.

How many lies would I have to tell to keep me out of Heaven?

I know I've lied more than once; have you ever told a lie?

★ If your friend doesn't agree, show him the context of Revelation 21:27 is Heaven (21:10–27) and Hell (20:10–15; 21:8).

Read the verse together. Does this verse indicate that telling just one lie keeps us from Heaven?

The real question is "What is God teaching us in this verse?" not "What is my interpretation or yours?"

If he still doesn't believe this concept, try to come to agreement about what the Bible teaches.

★ Disbelieving a truth doesn't change the truth.

Remember the list we discussed on page 7? Will even the smallest sins be allowed into Heaven?

What does the Bible say about our good works? (Even the good or righteous things we do are seen as filthy rags from God's holy perspective.)

How did you answer question 13?

How did you answer question 14?

How did you answer question 15?

★ Discuss the answer to question 15 together. Be sure to ask, "Anything else?"

THE EXCHANGE

Because God is holy, He cannot tolerate that which is not holy. We may think to ourselves that we can compensate for our sins by doing good things.

12. What does the Bible say that our good things are in the sight of our perfect God?

> Isaiah 64:6 But we are all as an unclean thing, and **all our righteousnesses [good things] are as filthy rags;** and we all do fade as a leaf; and our iniquities, like the wind, have taken us away.

_____

13. There is more to it than this, but if this were all you knew about God and men, who would make it to Heaven?

_____

14. Are you 100% sure that all your sins are forgiven and that you're going to Heaven?

_____

15. What do you think it takes to have a relationship with God and live with Him forever in Heaven?

_____

Think about this for a moment and record anything else that you think a person needs to depend on to get to Heaven.

_____

_____

God Is Holy

Lessons 3 and 4 deal with what the Bible has to say about these questions. If you don't want to wait until then to find out, feel free to ask your Bible study leader to show you from the Bible now.

SUMMARY

In John 8:31–51 Jesus is preaching about sin and its consequences. He told the crowd that if they would listen to the truth, the truth would set them free. The people to whom He was speaking took exception to the thought that they needed freedom. They saw themselves as free to do whatever they wanted to do and as answerable to no one. Jesus replied, "Verily, verily, I say *to* you, *whoever commits* sin is a servant [slave] of sin."

You may be as those men and see yourself as free from the constraints of this kind of teaching. Once I was talking with a man about this topic, and he somewhat sarcastically asked me, "How do you know this is true?"

I replied that the Bible is true and tells us more about ourselves than we can discover by personal observation. I told him the Bible teaches that all men are slaves to sin; and that everyone has an area of his own life that he knows is wrong but can't change because he is enslaved to it. By way of personal application I added, "Right now, there are probably things you do that you know are wrong and would like to stop doing, but you can't."

His glance in my direction told me that I had touched on something personal. He didn't even turn his head toward me, as if he suspected I was reading his mind. He responded by asking simply, "Everyone?"

I wasn't reading his mind. I had read the Bible. No man has the ability to overcome sin, but Jesus has made it clear that He is the Truth and **He can free us from the guilt and the control of sin**. What about you? Do you struggle with a sin that you know is wrong but you can't seem to quit? How do you deal with the guilt? Would you like to be free from sin and guilt once and for all? You can be, and this Bible study can lead you to the biblical truth of real freedom, so keep reading!

The first step to freedom is to admit that you are a slave. That is, that you are a sinner who has offended God and you cannot solve this problem

Jesus said, "Whoever commits sin is the slave of sin." Is there a sin that you feel guilty about and wish you could quit? (Consider sharing the feelings of guilt you have experienced. If you want your friend to be transparent, your personal transparency will help him feel safe.)

11

In the story of the religious man and the tax collector which of these men was sinful? (Both)

Describe the difference between the two men's responses? (The religious man was blind to sin. The tax collector was ashamed of sin.)

What was the result of their respective attitudes? (The religious man was no closer to God. The tax collector was forgiven.)

Make sure your friend understands the main point: *God is holy. Because I am sinful I am alienated from God.*

Would you like me to show you what the Bible says about going to Heaven, or would you rather study it for yourself in the next three lessons?

The next lesson deals with the justice of God, a pretty tough subject for most people. Lesson 3 is about the good news of God's love, so you can look forward to the "good news" while studying the "bad news" found in lesson 2.

THE EXCHANGE

by yourself. In Luke 18:9–14 Jesus told a story to some who trusted in themselves that they were righteous, and treated others with contempt.

He told of two men that went to the temple to pray. One of them was a very religious man, and the other was a tax collector. (The tax collectors of the day were despised for their personal greed and corruption.) The religious man stood in a prominent place with his eyes and hands lifted heavenward and prayed, "God, I thank you that I am not like other men, extortioners, unjust, adulterers, or even like this tax collector. I fast twice a week; I give tithes of all that I get."

The tax collector awkwardly stood some distance away and was not even willing to lift his face to Heaven. His actions and stance told of the sense of guilt he carried. He prayed simply, "God, be merciful to me, a sinner!"

Jesus then told His listeners that the man who had humbled himself before God went away justified rather than the religious man who had exalted himself. Gaining freedom from sin is not about trying harder or being better. It's too late for that, even if we could. It's about recognizing our need and admitting it to God!

APPLICATION

If you were going to talk to God about what you have learned in this Bible study lesson, what would you tell Him?

_____

_____

_____

MEMORIZE

Romans 3:23 For all have sinned, and come short of the glory of God.

12

PRACTICAL ASSIGNMENT

In the space provided, record any questions you may have so you can discuss them with your Bible study leader when you meet.

_____

_____

_____

_____

_____

_____

_____

_____

_____

_____

_____

If you would like to study some on your own, try reading a chapter in the book of John each day. Ask God to speak to you as you read His book. Since He is real, He can do that. He promises that He will convince you in your heart of certain truths about Himself and about you. He will not speak in an audible voice, but you will have a growing awareness that what the Bible says is true! You may even sense a tugging or a squeezing in your heart. That is the Lord!

In the space remaining, record any verses that seem to stand out to you or any questions you have as you read.

_____

_____

13

LESSON 1 REVIEW

God is holy.

- He cannot sin.

- He requires holiness from us.

God cannot deal with man in a way that is contrary to His nature.

God's Word is our final authority.

The Ten Commandments are a reflection of God's nature.

Example: "You shall not kill [murder]"—God is the creator and sustainer of life.

Who has sinned? (Everyone)

Reflect on the story of the religious man and tax collector. The religious man was blind to his sin and left the temple still alienated from God. The tax collector was humble and God forgave him.

⚖️ God Is Just

In lesson 1 we focused on the holiness of God. We learned that because God is holy, He cannot tolerate sin. This lesson focuses on His justice. This is not about a concept called justice but about a Person Whose nature is just. We will learn that because He is just, He cannot ignore or overlook our sin. As the just judge of all the earth, He must judge our sin.

1. In your own words describe the character of God shown in the following verse.

   > Deuteronomy 32:4 He is the Rock, his work is **perfect:** for all his ways are **judgment:** a God of **truth** and **without iniquity, just** and **right** is he.

   _____

He is the Rock, our perfect God, Whose every action is just. His very character is faithful and true without any error, and He is always just and right. Remember, He is perfect. He doesn't make any mistakes or commit any wrongs!

2. In the next lesson we will see that Jesus is God come to earth in a human body. What does this verse tell us about Him?

   > Hebrews 13:8 Jesus Christ **the same yesterday, and to day, and for ever.**

   _____

He never changes. His character is the same in every situation.

15

What do you think of the Bible study so far?

What questions do you have?

What did you learn that you didn't already know?

What impacted you most in this lesson?

How would you distinguish the difference between justice as a concept and a person whose nature is just?

How does God's unchanging nature affect your life? (Though our culture's view of right and wrong may change, God's standard of holiness never changes and His promises never change.)

Have you ever had a close friend grow distant or perhaps even betray you? God never changes. He will always be a loyal friend.

THE EXCHANGE

3. How is Jesus described in this verse?

> Acts 3:14 *You* denied the **Holy** One and the **Just.**

_____

4. Since God's nature is just, what can you expect from His actions?

> Psalm 111:7 The works of his hands are **verity [truth] and judgment [justice]; all his commandments are sure.**

_____

He is a just God. Not only does He act justly Himself, but He demands justice from men. We learned in lesson 1 that God's laws reflect His holy nature. God's justice is also reflected in many of His laws.

What words are used to describe God's justice? (do right, deal justly, judgment, one manner of law for the foreigner as well as the native)

5. Did God have one set of laws for foreigners and another for His own people? Why?

> Leviticus 24:22 *You* shall have **one manner of law,** as well for the stranger [foreigner], as for one of your own country: **for I am the** LORD **your God.**

_____

6. What words in this verse describe God's judgments?

What is God called in Genesis 18:25? (Judge of all the earth)

> Genesis 18:25 Shall not the Judge of all the earth **do right [deal justly]?**

_____

The topic of discussion in this passage is judgment, and the person who made this statement knew that he could count on God to deal with the judgment of the city in question in a just manner.

16

7. A covenant is a lasting promise or vow made with an oath. How does God's just nature affect His covenants positively and negatively?

> Deuteronomy 7:9–10 Know therefore that the Lord *your* God, he is God, the **faithful God, which *keeps* covenant** and mercy with them that love him and keep his commandments to a thousand generations; And ***repays* them that hate him to their face,** to destroy them: he will not be slack to him that *hates* him, he will repay him to his face.

Positively _____

Negatively _____

His unchanging, just nature is a blessing. We can look at every promise in the Bible and know that God will keep each one because He is just. However, His just nature is also a terrifying truth because He must repay every sin and every one of us is a sinner.

8. We learned in lesson 1 that the first impact of seeing God on His throne is His holiness. What else is true about the throne room of God?

> Psalm 89:14 **Justice and judgment are the habitation of *your* throne:** mercy and truth shall go before *your* face.

_____

9. What is God prepared to do? ←

> Psalm 9:7–8 But the Lᴏʀᴅ shall endure for ever: **he *has* prepared his throne for judgment.** And he shall judge the world in righteousness, he shall minister judgment to the people in uprightness.

_____

How did you answer question #7?

What is God prepared to do right now? (He's prepared to judge sinners.)

According to the Bible what will happen to the person who sins? (The soul that sins will die.)

How many sins will God allow into Heaven? (not even one)

Imagine a world where each person determined right from wrong. What would it be like? (Chaos would rule.)

THE EXCHANGE

10. What does God say will happen to the person who sins?

Ezekiel 18:20 **The soul that *sins*, it shall die.** The son shall not bear the iniquity of the father, neither shall the father bear the iniquity of the son: the righteousness of the righteous shall be upon him, and the wickedness of the wicked shall be upon him.

11. How many sins is God prepared to allow into Heaven?

Revelation 21:27 And **there shall in no wise enter into it [Heaven] any thing that *defiles*,** neither *whoever works* abomination, or *makes* a lie: but they which are written in the Lamb's book of life.

12. Who is the ultimate judge of equity?

Ezekiel 33:20 Yet *you* say, The way of the Lord is not equal ... **I [God] will judge** you every one after his ways.

Psalm 7:8 **The Lord shall judge** the people.

13. Someone might say, "I've done many good things in my lifetime," or "I've been a very religious person. Surely God will look at me differently because of my good works." What does God say about the way He judges?

Deuteronomy 10:17–18 For the Lord your God is God of gods, and Lord of lords, a great God, a mighty, and a terrible, which *regards* **not persons,** nor *takes* reward [bribes]: He *executes* judgment [justice].

18

Acts 10:34 **God is no respecter of persons.**

_____

14. Someone else might say, "But I didn't know about this!" What does the Bible say about this plea?

Proverbs 24:12 If _you say_, Behold, we knew it not; _does_ not he that _ponders_ the heart consider it? and he that _keeps your_ soul, _does_ not he know it? and **shall not he render to every man according to his works?**

_____

The concept of every man being judged "according" to his own actions occurs many times throughout the Bible. God will hold each of us accountable for the specific sins that we have done—not any that others have done, but all that we have done—whether we have been aware of those sins or not.

One person might say, "That's not fair." There is a difference between justice and fairness. Frankly, fairness is most often determined by feelings. Justice is determined by facts. Most people in prison are there justly. They broke some law of the land and were held accountable to that law. They may not feel that they have been treated fairly, but that does not change the fact that justice has been served. Justice is not defined by what we feel or want but by fixed laws or facts. One definition of _justice_ is "the administration of law." Just as God is holy and cannot tolerate sin, He is also just and cannot ignore it.

Another might say, "I thought God was a loving God. How can He judge people?" Imagine a judge presiding over a murder trial. A mountain of evidence proves that the defendant is guilty.

Would justice be served if the judge chose to overlook the obvious guilt and acquit the murderer? _____

19

★ In the story of the religious man and the tax collector, was God a respecter of persons? (No)

Is ignorance of God's nature an excuse?

★ A speeding violation is one example. Even if you didn't see the speed limit sign, you are held responsible.

We are not held responsible for someone else's sins—only our own.

What is the difference between fairness and justice? (Fairness is based on feelings. Justice is based on facts.)

What are your thoughts about the illustration of the judge and the murderer?

Do you remember this principle—"Love for the guilty does not change the demand for justice"? What illustration was used to clarify this point? (the judge and the murderer)

Would God be just if He overlooked your sin? (No! God, by His very nature, is bound to justice. He must judge our sin.)

THE EXCHANGE

If the guilty man was the judge's brother and he loved him very much, would it be just if the judge chose to overlook his guilt and acquit him? _____

God's love for the guilty does not change the demand for justice.

15. If God were to overlook **your** sin, would that be justice?
God is loving, but because of His nature He is bound by justice. He must judge our sin.

16. What does the Bible say we deserve because of our sin?

Romans 6:23 For the wages of sin is **death.**

_____

17. What kind of death is named in this description of the final judgment of men?

Revelation 20:11–14 And I saw a great white throne, and him that sat on it, from whose face the earth and the heaven fled away; and there was found no place for them. And I saw the dead, small and great, stand before God; and the books were opened: and another book was opened, which is the book of life: and the dead were judged out of those things which were written in the books, according to their works. And the sea gave up the dead which were in it; and death and hell delivered up the dead which were in them: and they were judged every man according to their works. And death and hell were cast into the lake of fire. **This is the second death.**

_____

This second death is most commonly called Hell or Hades. During Jesus' earthly ministry He spoke more about Hell than He spoke about Heaven. Some people believe that Hell is not a place but a state of mind or a figment of one's imagination.

20

Notice the words "according to what they have done" in Revelation 21:11-15. This phrase is used twice.

Why do you think Jesus spoke more about Hell than Heaven? (He doesn't want anyone to go to Hell. We often fail to accept the reality of Hell.)

18. Note the words the Bible uses to describe this awful place of judgment. Does it sound like a real place to you?

> Hebrews 9:27 It is appointed unto men once to die, but after this the **judgment.**

> Matthew 25:41, 46 Then shall he say also unto them on the left hand, Depart from me, *you* cursed, into **everlasting fire,** prepared for the devil and his angels.... And these shall go away into **everlasting punishment:** but the righteous into life eternal.

> Luke 3:17 ... will burn with **fire unquenchable.**

What are some words the Bible uses to describe the final judgment of men? (Hell, lake of fire, second death, judgment, everlasting fire, everlasting punishment, fire unquenchable, torments)

★ Remember in lesson 1 when we visualized Heaven and the angels calling out "Holy! Holy! Holy!"? It is almost unthinkable to visualize Hell.

Read this story told by Jesus. Doesn't Hell sound like a real place that should be avoided at all cost?

> Luke 16:19–24 There was a certain rich man, which was clothed in purple and fine linen, and fared sumptuously [lived splendidly] every day: And there was a certain beggar named Lazarus.... And it came to pass, that the beggar died, and was carried by the angels into Abraham's bosom: the rich man also died, and was buried; And in hell he lift up his eyes, **being in torments,** and *saw* Abraham afar off, and Lazarus in his bosom. And he cried and said, Father Abraham, have mercy on me, and send Lazarus, that he may dip the tip of his finger in water, and cool my tongue; for **I am tormented in this flame.**

Remember, God is no respecter of persons. He doesn't play favorites or place more value on wealthy people than poor people.

As terrible and unthinkable as it is, Hell is a real place.

19. Who does the Bible say will go into the lake of fire?

> Revelation 21:8 But the fearful, and unbelieving, and the abominable, and murderers, and whoremongers, and sorcerers, and idolaters, and **all liars, shall have their part in the lake** which *burns* with fire and brimstone: which is the second death.

Have you ever read a description of Hell? What did you notice about Hell from Luke 16:19-24?

1. The rich man is still aware, even after his death.

2. He was immediately in torment.

3. He longed for mercy but didn't get it.

4. He was physically thirsty.

5. His torment was physical.

21

How did you answer question 20?

★ If your friend answers "Hell," then ask him if he is concerned about this.

THE EXCHANGE

This is a rough list and maybe you're thinking you haven't done most of those things, but **have you ever told a lie**? How many murders does a man have to commit before he becomes a murderer? Only one. How many lies does a person have to tell before he becomes a liar? Only one.

You may be saying, "Wait a minute! I thought God is a God of love! How could a loving God do this?" Don't forget. God cannot deal with man in a way contrary to His nature. He is holy. He cannot tolerate sin. He is just. He cannot overlook sin. He must judge it, but God's love will not allow Him to ignore our doom. He has provided another way that satisfies His holiness, justice, and His love. This is the GOOD NEWS *The Exchange* is designed to tell you about. Lesson 3 deals with this good news, but before we move on, answer this most important question.

20. Based on what we have learned from the Bible so far, if you were to die right now, where would you go?

_____

If you had to honestly answer "Hell," are you concerned about this?

_____

Please don't be angry with God. Remember, He is just. He is doing what is right.

21. Who is at fault in this situation?

> Nehemiah 9:33 Y*ou* [God] *are* just in all that is brought upon us; for *you have* done right, but **we have done wickedly.**

_____

22. Dear friend, God doesn't want you to go to Hell! What does He want you to do right now?

> Ezekiel 18:32 For I have no pleasure in the death of him that *dies*, *says* the Lord God: wherefore **turn yourselves, and live.**

Do you think Jesus would rather condemn you or save you from this judgment?

If your house were on fire while you were sleeping, would you want someone to wake you and tell you about the fire?

Lessons 3 and 4 deal with what one has to do to "turn and live." If you don't want to wait until then to find out, feel free to ask your Bible study leader to show you from the Bible now.

SUMMARY

You might say, "This is frightening. Why would you focus on this?" Look at it this way. If I were standing on a dark mountain highway late on a stormy night and knew there was a bridge out just around the corner and I saw a car unknowingly speeding toward impending doom, what should I do? I must stop the car to warn the people inside of their danger! The danger of Hell is real and the warning is necessary!

In the illustration of the car on a road to impending doom, what if I didn't believe that those who warned me were telling the truth? (It would still be true. If I ignored the warning, I would still drive to my doom.)

I know a woman who knew these truths but kept putting off the decision to deal with her sins. She woke up one morning having dreamed about being in Hell. That was all it took! Fearful, she called her brother and begged him to come immediately to help her. When he arrived, she prayed the prayer of the tax collector in lesson 1. The fear that was so real a minute before rolled away and God gave her lasting peace.

Jesus has provided a way for cleansing and complete forgiveness. He is looking for people who will humble themselves before Him to save them from their doom. "*For the Son of man [Jesus] is come to seek and to save that which was lost*" (Luke 19:10).

Early one morning during Jesus' earthly ministry, some men dragged a weeping woman into the courtyard where He was teaching. They wanted to use her to catch Him in a trap. They told Him that she had been caught in the very act of adultery and that the Law demanded that she be stoned to death. They asked Him, "What do you have to say about that?"

23

In the story of the woman caught in adultery, was there any person who was without sin?

Could Jesus overlook the sins of the woman?

Could He overlook the sins of her accusers?

Can He overlook our sins?

Is He willing to forgive our sins?

Make sure your friend understands the main point: *God is Just. Because of my sin, I deserve God's condemnation.*

How does your understanding of God's justice change your view of where you'll spend eternity?

The next 2 lessons deal with what someone has to do to "turn and live." I can show you now how you can be sure you're going to heaven, or we can wait till you've studied more.

The next lesson deals with the love of God. It is the beginning of the good news. I hope you enjoy it as much as I do!

THE EXCHANGE

They knew that if He spoke contrary to the Jewish law, the Jews would lose respect for Him. If He condemned her, He would break the Roman law that forbad executions without Rome's consent and He would be arrested. There was a silent moment as the crowd of triumphant men waited for Him to walk into their inescapable trap.

Unexpectedly, He stooped and began to write in the dust with His finger. No one knows for sure what He wrote, but in that He knows everything, perhaps He began to list all of their hidden sins. He rose then and responded to their continued demand for an answer. "Which one of you is without sin? Let him be the first to throw a stone at her."

Then He silently stooped to write again, perhaps writing their more grievous and embarrassing sins. The Bible records that being convicted in their consciences about their own sins, they began to slip out one by one, beginning from the oldest to the youngest, until there was not one of them left but the accused woman.

Jesus rose from the ground and asked her, "Where are the witnesses against you? Is there no one to accuse you?"

With her head bowed to the ground in humility she answered, "No one, Lord," implying that she respected Him as judge and that her own heart told her that she was guilty. Jesus readily accepted her humble response and admonished her to "go and sin no more."

Jesus, the just Lord, was not willing to overlook the sins of her accusers and was willing to forgive her sins. Indeed, today He cannot overlook our sins, but He will gladly forgive those who will "turn and live."

APPLICATION

If you were going to talk to God about what you have learned in this Bible study, what would you tell Him?

_____

_____

_____

24

MEMORIZE

Romans 6:23 The wages of sin is death; but the gift of God is eternal life through Jesus Christ our Lord.

PRACTICAL ASSIGNMENT

In the space provided record any questions you may have so you can discuss them with your Bible study leader when you meet.

_____

_____

_____

If you would like to study some on your own, try reading a chapter in the book of John each day. Ask God to speak to you as you read His book. Since He is real, He can do that. He promises that He will convince you in your heart of certain truths about Himself and about you. He will not speak in an audible voice, but you will have a growing awareness that what the Bible says is true! You may even sense a tugging or a squeezing in your heart. That is the Lord!

In the space remaining, record any verses that seem to stand out to you or any questions you have as you read.

_____

_____

_____

_____

_____

_____

_____

_____

25

LESSON 2 REVIEW

God is holy and cannot tolerate our sin.

- He cannot sin.

- He requires holiness from us.

God is just and cannot overlook our sin.

- He is no respecter of persons.

- He cannot deal with a man in a way that is contrary to His nature.

- Man is sinful, and God cannot allow any sin into Heaven.

- Our good works cannot compensate for our sin.

- We deserve death because of our sin.

- Review what death is: judgment, second death, Hell, lake of fire, everlasting punishment.

Lesson
3

♡ God Is Loving

What we have learned about God in lessons 1–2 is awesome and true but it is bad news for mankind. God is holy and cannot tolerate our sin. He is just and cannot overlook our sin. Our sinful nature is offensive to His nature, and we are separated from Him and His perfection. If this were all there was to His nature, we would all be doomed. But there is more! The Bible teaches that "God is love" (1 John 4:8). While God cannot deny His nature and embrace us in our sin, He has provided a way for us to be close to Him because of His strong love for us. This perfect way to God satisfies His holiness and justice. Lesson 3 shows His great love and the provision He has made for us to enter into an eternal love relationship with Him.

1. We have all experienced the need for love. Does prosperity satisfy this need?

   > Ecclesiastes 5:10 **He that** *loves* **silver shall not be satisfied with silver;** nor he that *loves* abundance with increase: this is also vanity [empty living].

   _____

2. This proverb paints a contrasting picture of a feast or a sparse meal. Maybe you remember a meal that was perfect in every way except for arguing or bitter silence. Briefly record your experience.

   > Proverbs 15:17 Better is a dinner of herbs [sparse meal] **where love is,** than a stalled ox [feast] and **hatred therewith.**

   _____
   _____
   _____

27

What do you think of the Bible study so far?

What questions do you have?

What did you learn that you didn't already know?

What impacted you most in this lesson?

What would your life be like without love?

Does money satisfy our human need for love?

This may be hard for your friend to discuss. Share an experience from your own life before you ask him to share one of his.

What would you say is the most powerful motivation to the human mind?

Has there ever been a circumstance in your life when, out of love for someone, you did something that was hard to do?

Will there be faith in Heaven?

Will there be hope in Heaven?

Will there be love in Heaven?

Love is the greatest because love will survive time.

According to our Bible study, what does the ennobling human grace of love reflect? (the nature of our loving God)

THE EXCHANGE

We all have a deep need in our heart for love, and sometimes even the people we are closest to let us down. As you continue to read this lesson, you will learn that God intends to meet that need in your life through a loving relationship with Him.

What would you say is the most powerful motivation to the human mind? Some would say fear, citing the body's almost superhuman reactions to fear as evidence. Others would say greed or hunger for power, citing the inhumane atrocities that have been perpetrated because of these motives. I would propose that the greatest human motivation is love. Men have left all they have ever known and held dear for love of country and freedom. A close friend of mine ran into her burning house to save the life of her two-year-old daughter, resulting in burns to 65 percent of her body.

3. First Corinthians 13 is known as the Love Chapter. What does the last verse of that great chapter say about love?

1 Corinthians 13:13 And now *abides* faith, hope, charity [love], these three; but **the greatest of these is charity [love].**

Love is the most ennobling human grace because we reflect the character of our Creator. God is love, and He created us with a capacity and a need for love.

4. What did God say about His love for us, and what has He done about it?

Jeremiah 31:3 The LORD *has* appeared of old unto me, saying, Yea, **I have loved *you* with an everlasting love: therefore with lovingkindness have I drawn *you*.**

Hosea 11:4 **I [God] drew them** with cords of a man, **with bands of love.**

28

Even now, God is drawing you to Himself in love. Won't you open your heart to Him? God created all of us with an appetite for His love that cannot be satisfied with anything but an intimate love relationship with Him.

How have you sensed God drawing you to Himself lately?

5. How is God described in this passage?

> 2 Corinthians 13:11 Finally, brethren ... **the God of love and peace** shall be with you.

_____

6. Is God's love available to you?

> 2 Corinthians 13:14 The grace of the Lord Jesus Christ, and **the love of God,** and the communion of the Holy Ghost [Spirit], **be with you all.** Amen.

> 2 Thessalonians 3:5 And **the Lord direct your hearts into the love of God.**

_____

7. From these verses what benefits of His love speak to your heart?

What benefits of God's love touched your heart?

> Ephesians 3:19 And to know **the love of Christ, which** *passes* **knowledge, that** *you* **might be filled with all the fulness of God.**

> 2 Thessalonians 2:16-17 Now our Lord Jesus Christ himself, and God, even our Father, which *has* **loved us,** and *has* **given us everlasting consolation [comfort] and good hope through grace,** comfort your hearts, and stablish you in every good work.

_____

_____

Whom does God love?

★ Make sure your friend personalizes this answer: "God loves me!"

Notice the tension between God's love for sinners and His demand for purity and justice. This tension is what demanded God's extreme solution for our sin.

THE EXCHANGE

8. Whom does God love?

Deuteronomy 7:8 The LORD loved **you.**

_____

If you said "everyone," you are right, but the point is that He loves *you*, personally!

9. According to the Bible, where do we get our human capacity to love?

1 John 4:19 **We love** him [God], **because he first loved us.**

_____

10. Does the Bible indicate that God wants men to be separated from Him for eternity?

2 Peter 3:9 **The Lord is** not slack concerning his promise, as some men count slackness; but is longsuffering to us-ward, **not willing that any should perish,** but that all should come to repentance.

1 Timothy 2:4 **Who will have all men to be saved,** and to come unto the knowledge of the truth.

_____

God's love and God's holiness and justice seem to be in conflict regarding man's status. Yet they cannot be because God is perfect. The great love of God led Him to the most amazing act of love ever. He sent His own dear Son to bear our sin penalty for us.

11. What does the Bible say about true friendship?

Proverbs 17:17 **A friend *loves* at all times.**

_____

30

God Is Loving

12. Whom do you think this verse is talking about?

| Proverbs 18:24 **There is a friend** that *sticks* closer than a brother.

_____

God calls us His friends. How does this truth impact you?

Have you ever sinned?

Is God your friend?

Jesus said of Himself in John 15:13, "Greater love *has* no man than this, that a man lay down his life for his friends."

13. What was Jesus called by the men of His own time?

| Matthew 11:19 The Son of man came eating and drinking, and they say, Behold... **a friend of publicans and sinners.**

_____

14. In these verses, what motivated God to deliver His people?

| Isaiah 38:17 Behold, for peace I had great bitterness: but *you* [God] *have* **in love to my soul** delivered it from the pit of corruption: for *you have* cast all my sins behind *your* back.

| Isaiah 63:9 In all their affliction he [God] was afflicted [grieved]... **in his love and in his pity** he redeemed them; and he bare them, and carried them all the days of old.

_____

What motivates God to deliver people from sin? (love and pity)

The word *redeemed* paints a wonderful word picture. Because of their sin, God's people were taken captive and held as slaves. Out of His love and pity, God purchased them and set them free.

15. What does the Bible say God's love motivated Him to do?

| John 3:16 For God so loved the world, that **he gave his only begotten Son,** that *whoever believes* in him should not perish, but have everlasting life.

31

★ Even though I have offended God's holiness and earned His judgment, He chose to love me and give His only Son to die in my place.

★ You need to know your friend's answer to this question – "Who would you say Jesus is?"

★ Jesus is the God of the universe in a human body.

THE EXCHANGE

Romans 5:8 But God *commended* [stretched forth] his love toward us, in that, while we were yet sinners, **Christ died for us.**

God is loving and has reached out to us, but even in His love God cannot do anything that would violate the rest of His nature. It was through the gift of Jesus that He provided a way for us to be close to Him that satisfies His holy, just nature.

16. Who would you say Jesus is?

If you said, "the Son of God," you are right, but think about this—God calls all true Christians His children. Is Jesus different from them? YES!

17. Who does this verse say Jesus is?

Matthew 1:23 Behold, a virgin shall be with child, and shall bring forth a son, and they shall call his name Emmanuel, which being interpreted is, **God** with us.

---

18. What did Jesus' disciple Thomas call Him?

John 20:28 And Thomas answered and said unto him, **My LORD and my God.**

---

19. Would it be robbery to God's glory for any man to claim to be God's equal?

---

20. Was it robbery for Jesus to claim to be equal with God? Why?

32

> Philippians 2:6–7 Who, being in the form of God, **thought it not robbery to be equal with God:** But made himself of no reputation, and took upon him the form of a servant, and was made in the likeness of men.

_____

It was not robbery because He is God. John 1:1–3 and verse 14 teach that Jesus is God and was in Heaven from the beginning of time.

GOD'S EXCHANGE

Jesus left the splendor and perfection of Heaven, took on the body of a man and lived on earth so that He could die as the perfect *substitute* for our sin penalty. When the Bible says, "God so loved the world," it means every man and woman in the world. Jesus became a man so that He could give His life in *exchange* for every person who has sinned.

Our Substitute

This means He loves you in particular and has given Himself as your substitute.

21. What did Jesus do with our sins?

> 1 Peter 2:24 **Who his own self bare our sins in his own body on the tree,** that we, being dead to sins, should live unto righteousness: by whose stripes [punishment] *you* were healed.

_____

22. Describe the exchange Jesus offered through His suffering. Why did He make such an exchange?

> 1 Peter 3:18 For Christ also *has* once suffered for sins, [a]**the just for the unjust,** [b]**that he might bring us to God.**

   a. _____

   b. _____

How did Christ pay the judgment we deserve? (He died on the cross in our place.)

In lesson 1 do you remember discussing our list of extreme sins and more common sins? Did Jesus die for even the worst sins we have committed?

Imagine the magnitude of all the sins of all mankind from creation on.

33

Describe your thoughts about putting your name on the Exchange Chart?

What did you think about crossing out your name and replacing it with Jesus?

What about putting your name in Jesus' place?

It's an awesome exchange isn't it?

THE EXCHANGE

As the holy, just God Who came in human flesh, He is the only One qualified to die in your place. He took your sins on Himself when He died on the cross.

Our Righteousness
He dealt with your sinful record thoroughly, but He also offers His own record to you as a perfect completion to His exchange.

23. Describe the nature of the exchange as it is referred to in this verse.

> 2 Corinthians 5:21 For **he [God]** *has* **made him [Jesus] to be sin for us,** who knew no sin; **that we might be made the righteousness of God in him.**

When we take His offer, we take His righteous record and meet His holy standard. Only then can God give us a home with Him in Heaven forever and still be just. Write your name in the blank below.

THE EXCHANGE

_____'s Record	Jesus' Record
✓ Lying	✓ Holy
✓ Stealing	✓ Just
✓ Coveting	✓ Accepted by God
✓ Alienated from God	✓ Free to live with God

Now cross out your name and write *Jesus*. Cross out Jesus' name on the other side of the chart and write your own.

This is the reality of the exchange He offers us! On the cross Jesus suffered as a lying, coveting thief in your place and offers you the freedom to have a full relationship with God as your Father, accepted by Him because of Jesus' holy, just nature.

34

God Is Loving

Our Full Payment

You may be thinking, "I see that, but surely I must do something!"

24. Does Christ's death cover all your past sins? ←

> 1 John 1:7 The blood of Jesus Christ his Son *cleanses* us from **all** sin.

_____

Does it cover all your present, and even future, sins?

_____

The Bible says **all**! Yes, it means all your sins. You may be saying to yourself, "Okay, but I still have to keep myself from sinning to stay forgiven. It can't mean my future sins." Think about this. All your sins were future when Jesus died. He forgave all your sins—past, present, and even future!

25. What did Jesus mean when He cried these words from the cross?

> John 19:30 When Jesus therefore had received the vinegar, he said, **It is finished:** and he bowed his head, and gave up the ghost [his spirit].

_____

The word *finished* in the original language is *tetelestai* and means "**Paid in full!**"

If it was paid in full, is there anything left for you to pay?

_____

No! Jesus paid it all for you! We can't provide anything to save ourselves from our own sin penalty. He did all that was necessary to save us!

35

Did Christ's death cover all of your sins? What about your future sins?

How do we know His payment was sufficient to meet our need? (Christ said, "It is finished." It is paid in full. His blood washes away all our sin—past, present, and future.)

What miracle three days after Christ's death proved His sacrifice was accepted by the Father? (the resurrection)

Do you believe that Christ died and rose again?

★ If your friend says yes, move on to the next question. If your friend answers no, turn to 1 Corinthians 15:1–9.

Explain the proof of the eyewitnesses.

Discuss the change in the cowardly disciples, especially Peter who denied Jesus during His trial but later powerfully preached on the day of Pentecost.

Tell the story of Saul the persecutor's transformation to Paul the apostle.

★ The difference between Jesus and others who claim to be God is that Jesus rose from the grave and conquered death.

THE EXCHANGE

26. What does the Bible say happened to Christ after He died for our sins?

1 Corinthians 15:3–4 Christ died for our sins ... **he was buried,** and ... **he rose again** the third day according to the scriptures.

27. Circle the words *He was seen* in the passage below, which refers to the time immediately following His resurrection. You should find them four times.

1 Corinthians 15:5–8 And that he was seen of Cephas, then of the twelve: After that, he was seen of above five hundred brethren at once; of whom the greater part remain unto this present, but some are fallen asleep [dead]. After that, he was seen of James; then of all the apostles. And last of all he was seen of me also, as of one born out of due time.

After Jesus arose from the grave He was seen by over 500 eyewitnesses. Jesus defeated death and delivered us from sin and its penalty. Through the resurrection Jesus proved He was powerful enough to win the victory over sin for us. His resurrection also proved that God was satisfied with His payment for our sins. He loves, much more than most people suspect, and His love is powerful enough to reach even you and me! It's true! Jesus really is God. He really did leave Heaven's splendor to be born of a virgin, live a perfect life, and die in your place. And it is true that He really rose from the grave, defeating sin, death, and Hell for you.

Do you believe this? _____

36

SUMMARY

When Jesus was on earth, He told a touching story that clearly shows God's love. It is the story of the prodigal son found in Luke 15:11–24. Many will identify with the son in this retelling of the story.

There was a very wealthy man who had two sons. The younger of the two came to his father one day and demanded his half of the inheritance he was sure he would get some day. No doubt the father was brokenhearted, but he did not attempt to force the young man to love him. He decided to divide his wealth between his two sons. It wasn't very long afterward that the youngest son liquidated his assets and took a trip far away from his home. Who knows why? Perhaps he was jealous of his brother, perhaps he was embittered by his father's insistence on rules; but whatever the case, he had his freedom and he was going to spend that freedom, and spend it he did.

Reports traveled back to the father that the wayward son was living one long riot—hiring prostitutes, buying friends, and wasting all his money. When the money was gone, there came a great famine that caused an economic depression in the region where he had traveled, and the young man was destitute. He couldn't find work, and when he did finally get a job slopping hogs, it didn't even pay enough for him to eat.

One day while he was feeding the pigs, he was so hungry he found himself daydreaming about how good it would be to have the hogs' slop to eat. It was at this low point that he "came to himself" and realized what a fool he had been. He began to talk to himself out loud. "How many servants does my father have? They have food to waste and here I am literally dying of hunger!" With resolve in his voice and hope in his heart for the first time in a long time, he said, "I'm going home to face Dad! I'll say to him, 'Dad, I've done wrong. I've sinned against God and against you. I don't deserve to be your son anymore, but if you'll have me, I'd like to become one of your servants.'"

Hearing himself say those words gave him the courage to take the first few steps. After that his heart was light as he hurried home.

Several days later, weak from hunger, he found himself only a mile from home. Just around the corner he would be able to see the front porch of

What touched you the most about the story of the prodigal?

Do you believe that God is "watching and waiting" for you to admit your sin and turn to Him?

Is there anyone whose sins are so numerous or shameful that God does not love him?

the giant old house. Now he was frightened. What would his father say? Would he accept his apology? With those last few thoughts he rounded the bend. He stopped in his tracks and allowed his hungry eyes to drink in the beautiful sight. There was the old tree and the place where he and his brother used to play, and there was the house! Oh, how good it all looked. And then his heart skipped a beat when he realized that there was someone standing on the porch. There was a wave, and a faltering move toward him, and then he heard it across the way. His father was calling out his name.

It was a long way across the huge estate, but his father was running toward him the best that he could. He rehearsed the words he was going to say one more time. He wasn't prepared for what happened next. He felt the loving embrace of his father as he fell on him. The feeling was so warm and secure. It was as if he were a little boy again and everything was okay. His weary soul luxuriated in the warmth of that embrace. He and his father reluctantly stepped back and stood at arms length looking each other over. There he was face to face with his father. There was an awkward silent moment, and finally he heard himself saying, "Dad, I've done wrong. I've sinned against God and against you. I don't deserve to be your son anymore, but if . . ."

His father interrupted him. What the son didn't know was that his father had been on that porch for days watching and waiting for this very moment. His heart was burning with compassion as he called to the servants, "Bring forth the best robe in the house and dress this boy in something proper; and bring a family ring. Put it back on his hand; and he'll need some shoes."

Standing there with tears streaming down his face, looking at the weak, emaciated form of his son, he added, "Bring out the fatted calf, and kill it. Let's eat, and be happy again, for this my son was dead, and is alive now. He was lost, and is found." The father, the son, and the whole house began to celebrate.

Friend, this is a picture of God's attitude toward **you**. Your sin and His perfect nature have driven you apart. He can't tolerate or overlook your sin, but He longs to forgive you through the substitutionary death of His own dear Son. He is watching and waiting for you to admit your sin and seek His forgiveness.

Lesson 4 deals with how to receive this forgiveness. If you don't want to wait until then, please ask your Bible study leader to show you from the Bible now.

APPLICATION

If you were going to talk to God about what you have learned in this Bible study, what would you tell Him?

_____

_____

_____

MEMORIZE

> John 3:16 For God so loved the world, that he gave his only begotten Son, that _whoever believes_ in him should not perish, but have everlasting life.

PRACTICAL ASSIGNMENT

Read these additional verses about God's love for you and write your own words of appreciation to Him.

> 2 Corinthians 5:14 For **the love of Christ _constrains_ us;** because we thus judge, that if one died for all, then were all dead.

> Galatians 2:20 I am crucified with Christ: nevertheless I live; yet not I, but Christ _lives_ in me: and the life which I now live in the flesh I live by the faith of **the Son of God, who loved me, and gave himself for me.**

Make sure your friend understands the main point: _God is loving and He loves me personally. Though He cannot tolerate or overlook my sins, He gave Himself in exchange for me._

Would you like me to show you what the Bible says about how to have your sins forgiven and go to Heaven, or would you rather study it for yourself in the next lesson?

The next lesson shows how you can have God's grace and forgiveness.

THE EXCHANGE

Ephesians 5:2 And walk in **love,** as Christ also *has* **loved us, and** *has* **given himself for us an offering and a sacrifice to God for a sweetsmelling savour [fragrance].**

1 John 3:1 **Behold, what manner of love the Father *has* bestowed upon us,** that we should be called the sons of God.

1 John 3:16 Hereby perceive we the **love of God,** because **he laid down his life for us.**

1 John 4:9 In this was manifested [demonstrated] **the love of God** toward us, because that **God sent his only begotten Son into the world,** that we might live through him.

1 John 4:10 Herein is **love,** not that we loved God, but that **he loved us, and sent his Son to be the propitiation** [satisfaction for justice] **for our sins.**

Revelation 1:5 And from **Jesus Christ,** who is the faithful witness, and the first begotten of the dead, and the prince of the kings of the earth. Unto him that **loved us, and washed us from our sins in his own blood.**

_____

_____

_____

_____

_____

In the space provided record any questions you may have so you can discuss them with your Bible study leader when you meet.

_____

_____

_____

_____

_____

_____

_____

_____

_____

_____

_____

_____

If you would like to study some on your own, try reading a chapter in the book of John each day. Ask God to speak to you as you read His book. Since He is real, He can do that. He promises that He will convince you in your heart of certain truths about Himself and about you. He will not speak in an audible voice, but you will have a growing awareness that what the Bible says is true! You may even sense a tugging or a squeezing in your heart. That is the Lord!

In the space remaining, record any verses that seem to stand out to you or any questions you have as you read.

_____

_____

_____

_____

_____

_____

Offer to answer any questions your friend may have had from the book of John.

What is your favorite passage so far?

41

LESSON 3 REVIEW

God is holy and cannot tolerate our sin.

- He cannot sin.

- He requires holiness from us.

God is just and cannot overlook our sin.

- Man is sinful, and God cannot allow any sin into heaven.

- Our good works cannot compensate for our sin.

- We deserve death because of our sin.

God is loving and has reached out to us.

- God initiates relationships with man.

- God does not want us separated from Him for eternity (2 Peter 3:9).

- God displayed His great love for man by sending His only Son to die for our sins.

- Jesus is God (Matthew 1:23).

- Jesus paid the penalty we deserve—death.

- Jesus offers forgiveness of sins through His exchange.

- Jesus offers us His righteousness.

- Jesus rose, victorious over death.

Lesson
4

⛐ God Is Gracious

So far we have seen that God is holy and cannot tolerate our sin, He is just and cannot overlook our sin, and He is love and cannot ignore our problem. His love compelled Him to send Jesus to live a perfect life and die in our place as payment for our sin. The transfer of this payment of sin can be applied to our need only through a gift. We can do nothing to earn it. This gift from God is called grace. This lesson is about the marvelous grace of God and how we can access His grace through faith.

1. God's holy and just nature keeps Him from simply clearing the guilty. What part of His character caused Him to seek a way to forgive our guilt?

   > Exodus 34:6–7 The LORD God, **merciful and gracious,** longsuffering [slow to anger], and abundant in goodness and truth, Keeping mercy for thousands, forgiving iniquity and transgression and sin, and that will by no means clear the guilty.

   _____

2. In lesson 2 we saw that God is prepared to judge our sin. What else is He ready to do? Why?

   > Nehemiah 9:17 *You are* **a God ready to pardon, gracious and merciful,** slow to anger, and of great kindness.

   _____

43

What do you think of the Bible study so far?

What questions do you have?

What did you learn that you didn't already know?

What impacted you most in this lesson?

Now that you have studied this lesson how would you define grace? (Grace is God giving to man what he does not deserve. Mercy is God not giving to man what he does deserve.)

THE EXCHANGE

Grace is God giving to man what he does not deserve. Mercy is God not giving to man what he does deserve. Do you remember what we deserve because of our sins?_____

3. God's love and mercy delivered the person who wrote Psalm 86 from an eternal consequence. What was it?

> Psalm 86:13 For great is *your* **mercy toward me: and** *you have* **delivered my soul from the lowest hell.**

_____

Why does God answer prayer? (because He is gracious and compassionate)

4. Why is God willing to hear our prayers?

> Exodus 22:27 And it shall come to pass, when he *cries* unto me, that I will hear; **for I am gracious.**

_____

God doesn't answer our prayers because we have been good, but because of His gracious nature.

How did God's grace become available to man? (through the substitutionary death and resurrection of Jesus)

Remember the illustration of the Grand Canyon? Jesus bridged the gap between God and man.

5. How did God's grace become available to mankind?

> John 1:17 For the law was given by Moses, but **grace** and truth **came by Jesus Christ.**

_____

6. To whom does God make His grace available?

> Titus 2:11 For **the grace of God** that *brings* salvation *has* **appeared [been made visible] to all men.**

_____

7. Grace was given to mankind as a gift from God. Who paid the price for God's grace?

44

2 Corinthians 8:9 For *you* know **the grace of our Lord Jesus Christ,** that, though he was rich, yet for your sakes he became poor, that *you* through his poverty might be rich.

_____

Do you see God's exchange in this verse? (He took our poverty on Himself and made us rich in His place.)

The exchange described in this verse is the same concept we learned about in lesson 3 now described through different words.

8. How do we gain access to the gift of God's grace?

Romans 5:1–2 Therefore being **justified by faith,** we have peace with God through our Lord Jesus Christ: By whom also we have **access by faith into this grace** wherein we stand, and rejoice in hope of the glory of God.

_____

How do we get God's free gift of grace? (by faith)

9. The words *faith* and *believe* mean the same thing. Record the promise associated with believing found in each of these verses.

Acts 10:43 Through his name *whoever believes* **in him shall receive remission [forgiveness] of sins.**

_____

Romans 10:4 For Christ is the end [fulfilment] of the law for **righteousness to every one that** *believes.*

_____

John 6:47 Verily, verily, I say unto you, **He that** *believes* **on me** *has* **everlasting life.**

_____

What does God promise to give to those who believe?

• forgiveness of sins

• Christ's righteousness credited to our account

• everlasting life

45

THE EXCHANGE

Christ provided forgiveness of sins, His perfect righteousness credited to our account, and eternal life in Heaven when He died and rose again. All this is available to each person on earth through God's grace and is accessed by faith. Since faith determines so much, it is necessary for us to define it clearly.

10. How would you define faith?

_____

COMMON FAITH

Many define faith as **understanding** or **acknowledging** that these things are true. Others might add that faith includes heart-felt agreement. While understanding these truths is foundational, it is not enough. I understand the premise of many things with which I do not agree. However, acknowledging Christ intellectually and even agreeing in your heart with what you know is true is still not enough.

11. Did the demons in this passage know and agree that Christ is the Son of God?

> Luke 4:41 And devils also came out of many, crying out, and saying, *You* [Jesus] *are* **Christ the Son of God. ... for they knew that he was Christ.**

_____

Demons understand that Jesus is the Son of God, Who died and rose again, and they agree with this reality; but obviously they are not on their way to Heaven.

God Is Gracious

SAVING FAITH

Faith that accesses God's grace and saves a person from sin and Hell has three essential elements. It's just like the angles of a triangle, or the legs of a three-legged stool, where every angle or leg is essential. Even so, saving faith is not saving if it is not complete. The first two angles of saving faith are found in common faith. (1) You must **understand** that God cannot tolerate or overlook your sin, that he gave His life in exchange for yours, and that He wants to give you eternal life. (2) You must also **agree** that you are a sinner who needs a Savior. The first two angles deal with the mind and emotions, but the third is a decision involving the will. (3) You must choose to **depend or trust** on Jesus Christ to forgive your sins and give you His righteousness, exchanging your sin and its penalty for His record and eternal life.

Describe the difference between common faith and saving faith.

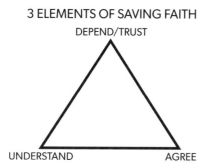

3 ELEMENTS OF SAVING FAITH
DEPEND/TRUST

UNDERSTAND   AGREE

In 1859, the famous acrobat Charles Blondin stretched a tightrope 190 feet above the waters of Niagara Falls. Crowds gathered daily as he navigated the thousand-foot span. He walked across in a large burlap bag. He carried his manager across on his back. He even fitted a special wheelbarrow for the rope and pushed it across. Once, he put a cookstove in the wheelbarrow and stopped in the middle of the rope to cook and eat an omelet. The story is told that once while working with the wheelbarrow, he approached the cheering crowd and asked them who **believed** he could put a man in the wheelbarrow and take him across. The crowd went wild. Everyone wanted to see that stunt. They began to chant, "I believe, I believe!"

47

Why was the man who was chanting, "I believe" not willing to get into the wheelbarrow? (Some might say he didn't really believe. Perhaps he did believe Blondin could take someone across, but he wasn't willing to trust Blondin to take him across.)

★ Missionary Gladys Aylward once fled civil unrest in China with over one hundred orphans. When she came to the Yellow River she looked at the expanse of water with despair. One of the children asked, "Do you believe the story of Moses?" At that moment she realized that the God Who parted the Red Sea for Moses could get her across the Yellow River. She had believed the story, but not until that moment did she realize that God's miraculous help was available to her. While she prayed for God's deliverance, a Chinese officer interrupted her. After realizing her plight, he signaled for a boat to carry her and the children across the river.

THE EXCHANGE

Blondin pointed to a man waving his hand and chanting, "I believe!" He said to the man, "You, sir, get in the wheelbarrow."

The man bolted in the other direction. What was wrong? The man might have believed that Blondin could put a man in the wheelbarrow—some other man—but he wasn't willing to **trust** Blondin to take **him** across.

This third angle of saving faith is the angle that many people neglect. They believe that Jesus lived and died and agree that this is good, but they still believe they need to do something to earn favor with God. They are depending on their good works. They believe they have to be good to their fellow man, try to obey God's law, and so forth.

12. Is it possible to satisfy God's holiness and justice through our own abilities?

> Romans 3:20 Therefore **by the deeds of the law there shall no flesh be justified** in his sight: for by the law is the knowledge of sin.

13. The law was given to show us that we are sinners and that we need a Savior. Where does the Bible say we find favor with God?

> Romans 3:24 Being **justified freely by his grace** through the redemption **that is in Christ Jesus.**

14. What conclusion does the Bible come to concerning the place of our own good works in receiving grace?

> Romans 4:4–5, 16 Now to him that *works* is the reward not reckoned of grace, but of debt. But to him that *works* not, but *believes* on him that *justifies* the ungodly, his faith is counted for righteousness. ...Therefore **it is of faith,** that it might be by grace.

God Is Gracious

15. Since receiving salvation from sin and death is by grace, then what is it not by?

> Romans 11:6 And if by grace, **then is it no more of works:** otherwise grace is no more grace.

_____

16. What are the two words that are involved in salvation from sin and Hell? Do either of these words involve anything **we** do?

> Ephesians 2:8–9 **For by grace are** *you* **saved** through faith; and that **not of yourselves:** it is the gift of God: **Not of works,** lest any man should boast.

> Titus 3:5 **Not by works** of righteousness which we have done, but **according to his mercy he saved us,** by the washing of regeneration, and renewing of the Holy Ghost [Spirit].

_____

_____

17. Some might still say they want to add their own good works to their faith just to be sure. What does the Bible say about adding works to what you depend on for salvation?

> Romans 3:28 Therefore we conclude that a man is **justified by faith without the deeds of the law.**

_____

Imagine two chairs sitting side by side. The one on the left represents you and your efforts to get to Heaven on your own, and the one on the right represents the finished payment of Christ for all your sins. If you are sitting in the chair representing self, what do you have to do to transfer your dependence to the chair representing Christ? You have to get out of the one chair and sit in the other. Similarly, you have to stop depending

49

Does salvation come from faith plus works? (The fact that the man trusts something other than Jesus shows a lack of trust in Jesus.)

What two words describe God's work in salvation from sin and Hell? (grace and mercy)

★ Walk through the two-chair illustration with your friend. If possible, use two chairs and demonstrate it.

If I say I've trusted in God to forgive my sins and give me eternal life, but I still try to do good works just in case, what does this indicate about my faith in Jesus' finished work on the cross? (This indicates that I don't think Jesus is enough.)

If I say I've always believed in God, what does that indicate about my faith? (There was no point of decision to depend on God. This kind of faith is only an acknowledgement of the facts. A volitional decision demands a point in time.)

★ Can a man say, "I've been married all my life." No. There had to be a point in time when he made a marriage vow to his wife.

on what you can do before you can transfer your trust to God's grace for salvation. It is a decision to trust Jesus alone to save you from your sins. Just like someone would have had to get in Blondine's wheelbarrow to demonstrate real dependence on his ability to take him across, even so you have to decide to trust Jesus alone to give you eternal life in Heaven.

What if a person decides to sit in both chairs? Is he really trusting either chair? No! When a person tries to trust in Jesus and his own efforts, he is really showing that he doubts that Jesus is enough. Saving faith is choosing to trust Christ's payment for sin as your own payment and nothing else. It's like a transaction or better—an exchange. You choose to trust Christ and what He has already done for you on the cross, and He gives to you forgiveness of sins (your earned record), His righteousness (His earned record), and eternal life.

18. What is another Bible word for this decision?

> Luke 13:3 I tell you, Nay: but, except *you* **repent,** *you* shall all likewise perish.

The word *repent* means to change your mind. Maybe you have been thinking that your sins are not bad enough to condemn you to Hell. You will have to change your mind about that. Perhaps you have been thinking that your own good works will outweigh your sins and get you to Heaven. You will have to change your mind about that. Maybe you've questioned if Christ's death on the cross was enough? You will have to change your mind about that. Simply admit, "God, You are right to condemn my sin; I'm the one who is wrong."

You must make a choice. Will you continue to trust in yourself and your own way, or will you transfer your trust to Jesus and what He has done to save you from your sin?

SUMMARY

There is a point of no return on the Niagara River, where the current from the falls is too powerful for a boat to navigate safely. It's marked clearly with warnings, because if a boat goes past that point, it is bound to be pulled by the current over the roaring falls. Imagine absentmindedly rowing a boat past that point. Suddenly you realize what you have done and try to turn back to safety, but it is too late. No matter how hard you row, you're still being pulled inch-by-inch closer to impending doom. Suppose someone on the shore sees your plight and expertly throws a rope across your lap. Now you have a choice to make. Will you keep up your own efforts only to eventually plunge to sure destruction, or will you drop the oars and trust the rope of safety?

The water is like your sin. It is pulling you to destruction. Those oars are like your own good works and religious activities. You may be working very hard, but your good works are not enough to save you. Your sin is too strong. Jesus is like that rope. He is your only hope of salvation from sin and Hell. What will you do with Jesus?

19. What does the Bible say is necessary to receive God's grace?

James 4:6 God *resists* [opposes] the proud, but **gives grace unto the humble.**

Will you humble yourself and admit that you have sinned and that your sin is an offense to our holy God? Will you admit that you can't save yourself from His justice? Will you humble yourself and trust the loving gift of His exchange, which He longs to give you? Will you humble yourself and place your dependence on Him and His finished work on the cross?

Please answer these questions carefully.

Do you believe that Jesus loves you and will save you from your sin and give you eternal life if you ask Him? _____

★ Tell your friend the story of when you put your trust in Jesus.

Has there ever been a time when you quit trusting in yourself and put your trust in Jesus alone?

If so, tell me about it.

★ If your friend has accepted Christ, encourage him to do the *Living the Exchange* Bible study with you.

How did you answer these two questions?

• Do you believe that Jesus loves you and will save you from your sins and give you eternal life if you ask Him?

• Then are you willing to follow Jesus and put your trust in Him right now?

51

★ If your friend is not trusting Christ, ask her if she would like to do so now?

The best way to do that is to tell Him in a prayer. Prayer is simply talking to God. Your friend can talk to God in her own words, or you might need to help her.

(If she chooses to pray silently, ask her to share with you what she just told God.)

★ If your friend just received Christ, go through questions 20–23 again for assurance.

She may need a little help understanding the reality of the decision she's made. Be patient and help her see the amazing difference Christ has made in her life.

★ Give your friend a copy of the "Living the Exchange" pamphlet found on page 57 of this Leader's Guide. This is designed for you to photocopy and fold as a four-page pamphlet to give to your friend. Go through the main points and encourage him to read it. Ask your friend to study *Living the Exchange* with you.

THE EXCHANGE

Then, are you willing to follow Jesus and put your trust in Him right now? _____

If your answer is yes, tell Him right now in a prayer.

Record below what you told Him.

_____

_____

_____

_____

_____

_____

_____

_____

Here is a sample prayer, but praying "just the right words" isn't what saves you. Your choice to depend on Jesus alone is what saves you from sin and its penalty. You can use this prayer as a guide or you can just talk to Him from your heart.

> Dear Jesus, I have sinned against Your holy nature and deserve judgment in Hell. I believe that You loved me enough to die in my place. Please forgive my sins, exchange my sinful record for Your holy one, and give me eternal life in Heaven. Right now, I place my dependence on You alone for salvation. Thank You, Jesus. Amen

20. Did you transfer your dependence to Jesus alone to save you from sin and Hell?

_____

52

21. Based on what you have seen in His Word, if you were to die right now where would you go? (Remember God cannot lie.)

_____

22. If you were to die five years from now, where would you go?

_____

It's not about what you feel or even what you think. It's about what God has promised. Look back at question 9 to see what He promised to do if you decide to believe. If you made the decision to depend on Him for grace, He has given you everlasting life. How long is everlasting? _____

Sometimes people answer these questions incorrectly. In that case, just work through these questions carefully.

23. How long will you have forgiveness of sins, righteousness, and eternal life?

_____

24. If you had died yesterday, or before you made this decision, where would you have gone?

_____

Remember, Revelation 20:14 says, "And death and hell were cast into the lake of fire. This is the second death." You see, this decision has made a huge difference, hasn't it?

25. Were you guilty before you made this decision?

_____

26. Are you guilty now?

Don't rely on your feelings. Put your trust in the Word of God.

_____

53

THE EXCHANGE

Remember the promises!

> Psalm 103:12 As far as the east is from the west, so far *has* he removed our transgressions from us.

South will meet north at the poles, but you can travel east for twenty years and you will never go west. They never meet! That is how far removed your guilt is! You have heard the Truth and the Truth has set you FREE!

APPLICATION

If you were going to talk to God about what you have learned in this Bible study, what would you tell Him?

_____

_____

_____

_____

MEMORIZE

> John 6:47 Verily, verily, I say unto you, He that *believes* on me *has* everlasting life.

PRACTICAL ASSIGNMENT

If you have made this decision, why don't you call your Bible study leader right now. This is cause for rejoicing!

Read these verses to see if you can determine Who else is rejoicing with you.

> Luke 15:7 I say unto you, that ... **joy shall be in heaven** over one sinner that *repents*, more than over ninety and nine just persons, which need no repentance.

54

Luke 15:10 Likewise, I say unto you, there is **joy in the presence of the angels of God** over one sinner that *repents*.

Luke 15:24 For this my son was dead, and is alive again; he was lost, and is found. And **they began to be merry.**

27. Who is in Heaven with the angels?

_____

Right now, God Himself is rejoicing that you have come home to Him.

In the space provided record any questions you may have so you can discuss them with your Bible study leader when you meet.

_____

_____

_____

_____

_____

_____

If you would like to study some on your own, try reading a chapter in the book of John each day. Ask God to speak to you as you read His book. Since He is real, He can do that. He promises that He will convince you in your heart of certain truths about Himself and about you. He will not speak in an audible voice, but you will have a growing awareness that what the Bible says is true! You may even sense a tugging or a squeezing in your heart. That is the Lord!

In the space remaining, record any verses that seem to stand out to you or any questions you have as you read.

If your friend trusted Christ, rejoice with him. This is his spiritual birthday!

_____

_____

_____

_____

_____

_____

LIVING THE EXCHANGE

Living the Exchange is a twelve-lesson Bible study that will help you grow in your new relationship with Christ. The Gospel provides far more than just eternal life in Heaven. Jesus offers victory over enslaving sins, peace and contentment in your daily life. As you learn to follow Him, He'll help you in practical aspects of everyday life—your job, family relationships, financial decisions, and so much more.

Jesus not only took your sin penalty but He gave you Himself! Everything that Christ is, He is in you! In *Living the Exchange* you'll learn to live out of the exchange He has made with you. Let's get started now.

56

The following two pages are designed to photocopy front and back and fold as a four-page booklet like a church bulletin. This invitation is provided to give to the person who has just completed T*he Exchange.* ⟶

LIVING THE EXCHANGE

When you received Jesus Christ as your Savior a vast inheritance became yours. Holocaust survivor Roman Blum moved to the United States, amassed a fortune and died at the age of 97 with no will and no surviving relatives. A $40 million inheritance was left to no one. Unlike Roman Blum, God has made His inheritance readily available to you and you can discover the riches of your inheritance in the pages of the Bible. *He has saved you from the penalty of sin; He is currently saving you from the power of sin; and He will some day save your from the very presence of sin* by giving you an eternal home in Heaven. The first and last of these gifts were automatically given to you, settled the moment you made your great exchange with God by trusting Jesus. The gift of the power to defeat sin in your life was also given to you at salvation, but you have to access this gift by faith. You might say this victory is in your spiritual "bank account." But you have to "write checks" against your account in order to have its benefits. Let's investigate your vast inheritance to see how you can come into full possession of all that is already yours in Christ.

Galatians 2:20 says it this way, "I am crucified with Christ: nevertheless I live; yet not I, but Christ *lives* in me: and the life which I now live in the flesh I live by the faith of the Son of God, who loved me, and gave himself for me." Before salvation you were unable to please God, but not anymore! When you trusted Christ, you died with Him. Just as Jesus rose from the grave, the Bible teaches that you rose with Him. When you received Jesus, you received LIFE (John 14:6) and He wants to live His life through you. You can live His life as you trust His promises and step out on them. "The just shall live by faith" (Romans 1:17).

HIS WORD

What you have read so far is only a glimpse of the gifts promised in the Bible that are now yours by inheritance in Christ. In fact, one of the greatest of these gifts is the Bible itself. It is your lifeline to Him. "As newborn babes, desire the sincere milk of the word, that *you* may grow thereby" (I Peter 2:2). Babies have an incredible appetite and an amazing capacity to grow. They are also susceptible to extreme health problems if they do not eat sufficiently. As a new Christian, in a spiritual sense this is true of you. As you choose to nourish yourself through reading, studying, memorizing, and hearing God's Word, you will receive His strength to keep growing in your relationship with God. If you neglect His Word, you are vulnerable to spiritual danger.

The Bible is more than a book. It's a library of books. John, the fourth book in the New Testament, is a great place to start. It is full of accounts of Jesus' life here on earth.

LIVING THE EXCHANGE

Living the Exchange is a twelve-lesson Bible study that will help you grow in your new relationship with Christ. The gospel provides far more than just eternal life in Heaven. Jesus offers victory over enslaving sins and peace and contentment in your daily life. As you learn to follow Him, He'll help you in practical aspects of everyday life—your job, family relationships, financial decisions, and so much more.

Jesus not only took your sin penalty but He gave you Himself! Everything that Christ is, He is in you! In *Living the Exchange* you'll learn to live out of the exchange He has made with you. Let's get started now.

ASSURANCE

You are completely safe in Jesus! "Verily, verily, I say unto you, He that *hears* my word, and *believes* on him that sent me, *has* everlasting life, and shall not come into condemnation; but is passed from death unto life" (John 5:24). Let's divide this verse into two simple parts.

YOUR RESPONSIBILITY

Jesus makes some amazing promises that are based on two conditions:
1. Did you learn the truth about salvation from sin from God's word? _____
2. Are you trusting God's greatest gift—Jesus Christ sent to die in your place? _____
If you have chosen to put your trust in Jesus then you can claim these three promises.

GOD'S PROMISES

The first promise is that *you have eternal life.* It isn't that you will have eternal life in the future. The Bible says you have it now, in your possession! How long does trust Jesus. When will your eternal life end? *Never*. You are eternally safe in Jesus.

The second promise Jesus makes is that *you will never come into condemnation*. In *The Exchange* you studied passages in the Bible that show the just judgment of God on those who are condemned to Hell. You will never come under that condemnation. You never need to worry about that again. You are safe in Jesus.

The third promise speaks of the tremendous change that has taken place in your life. You passed from spiritual death to spiritual life. Before you trusted Christ you had little desire and no ability to please God, but now *you have everything you need to fully please Him.* Jesus promised that "Heaven and earth shall pass away, but my words shall not pass away" (Matthew 24:35). God's Word is true at all times. You may not always feel your new freedom in Christ, but your feelings don't change the fact that you are now spiritually alive and have the ability to say no to sin and yes to God.

ACCEPTANCE

You are now fully accepted by God. "He *has* made us accepted in the beloved" (Ephesians 1:6). But we've sinned; how can we be accepted by God? Twice while Jesus was here on earth, God spoke from heaven, "This is my beloved Son, in whom I am well pleased" (Matthew 3:17; 17:5). God is holy! Jesus is the only human Who has ever completely pleased God because He alone is truly holy. When Jesus died, He fully paid for our sin and offered to exchange our sinful record for His holy record. You are as accepted by God as Christ is because you were placed into Christ's standing when you made your exchange with Jesus.

ADOPTION

NEW HEAVENLY FAMILY

You have been adopted into God's family. Romans 8:15 says, "For *you have not* received the spirit of bondage again to *fear*; but *you have* received the Spirit of adoption, whereby we cry, Abba, Father." *Abba* is an endearing word for father similar to our word *daddy*. God has given you the closest of all relationships— He's made you His child. His Holy Spirit now lives in you to help you want to call out to Him in time of need. You can make appeals to His throne as only a close family member can.

God has also given you a family here on earth to help you grow—your church family. God built the church to help you have a vibrant, zealous life. Picture a fire burning brightly in a cozy fireplace. What happens if you take a log out of the fire and set it on the hearth? No more cozy fire! That log will stop burning, start smoking and will make a mess. It loses its usefulness. If you return the log into the fire where it belongs, it will burn brightly and warm the room. God designed the church to help you stay on fire and useful for the Lord. Many times believers who neglect church lose their zeal and make a mess of God's plan for their lives. Christians who stay in church as God intended, can grow spiritually and in their usefulness to God.

Church is not only where you learn from God's Word, it's where you fellowship with other believers who are going through similar life experiences. No wonder God told us not to neglect church (Hebrews 10:25). He wants to give you lifelong friendships with people who will help you and whom you can help. God wants to give you a sense of belonging as well as a sense of purpose and fulfillment. It's often through church that we discover God's plan to use us to help build His eternal Kingdom. Why don't you decide right now to begin a pattern of faithful attendance in church? You'll be glad you did.

VAST INHERITANCE

You are only beginning to understand the fullness of God's love. You possess a vast inheritance now that you have Christ as your Savior. Your rights to this inheritance result from the exchange you made with Jesus—His righteous record in exchange for your sinful record, His victorious life in exchange for your spiritual death and inability to please God.

HIS VICTORY

"But thanks be to God, which *gives* us the victory through our Lord Jesus Christ" (1 Corinthians 15:57). God promises that there is not one temptation that comes into your life that He will not enable you to resist (1 Corinthians 10:13). Hard work and struggle are part of life on earth, but these alone are not enough to give you victory. Like salvation, you can't earn it. Victory is part of His gift of grace to you and is received by faith as part of your inheritance rights. It's like money placed into your spiritual "bank account." Victory is yours, but you live in victory moment by moment by looking to Jesus. "For therein is the righteousness of God revealed from faith to faith: as it is written, The just shall live by faith" (Romans 1:17).